Lion

New Poems

by
Tallas Munro

AOS PUBLISHING, 2024

AOS POETRY, 2024

ISBN: 978-1-990496-70-7

Cover Design: Chanelle Poupart

Visit AOS Publishing's website:
www.aospublishing.com

To everyone who helped make this possible.

For Keira.

Table of Contents

Silence

You are the subject of many silences.

Sensory

I feel the draft when the window is closed
sliding across my ankles.
Exhausts on my pillow
eyes crawl to yours,
you're my candle I walk through without being burned.
Fingertips weighing down over your skin
concentration melts in the
curiosity of a freckle.
An overgrowth of questions on my palette
swallowed in silent streams of your speech against mine.
How empty my name was
until I heard it through your sigh.

Freedom

Freedom blew through like a windswept dress on a mannequin
then I knew
I could be free too.

Cafuné

Asleep on my chest,
breeze of muscle memory ripples out of my fingers
plowing the line between familiar and nostalgic.
Your chest unhooks a long hanging moan
lifting my bottled breath between bone
out in speechless conversation.
Living our life outside
as it is inside.

Hurt

I think about you alone at night.
It hurts me more
than you with someone else.

Negotiations with Heat

Negotiations with heat
hitched my eye line
like a spark treads through a fuse.
You've introduced me to my knotted blood
red tape taboo
where the flexibility of flame
maneuvers the burn vein to vein.

We share an itch: different
but both beneath the skin
never just taking or leaving.
It's give, take, and come back later
to find that the only love that exists
shines on your skin.

It's as loveless
as hunger not telling me to eat,
drowsiness not closing my eyes,
and nothing
happening too quickly.

Maps

Laying out maps over the floor and dancing on top
was the closest we could get to traveling the world.

Farm

The birds lift the sun over the horizon,
lilacs with their heads hung low.
We trade hours for these seconds
starlight motivation for candlelight contentment
in this modest altar of rhubarb and savory.
Imperial innocence, absorbed rather than absorbing.
When soft, we soak
perspective changing our chemistry.

Clouds

Clouds are empty
you only know
after you've been through them.

Lion

Muse,
this is my first time hearing your voice
as the sacred line between
bloom and buried, rusting in dirt.

Flowering where touch
favors certainty,
as a tender pillow spoiled
by mire from your face
tempting rainfall
and renewing marsh libraries.

You speak in leaves applauding the performance of wind
calming keys turning before
we walk through the doorway valley.
Lion, now you are free!

Low Tide

If I were to kiss you,
I'd do it slow
to the pace of waves in low tide.

Curve

The edge curves itself as a smile
before you fall off.

Skyscraper

There's a skyscraper hanging off a cloud
I saw it in a puddle
before jumping over it
to see myself in the sky.

Year

For the past year or so,
the world and
me and you
have grown colder.
Just like a snowflake falling from the sky
me and you
falling through a storm
me and you
searching for a friend
me and you.

Moon

Does the moon know how bright it is
or does it long for the light of stars
like we do?

Bamboo Horse

Trots unbounded by rhyme
with the heart's muscled rhythm,
chase the end of the surf-tormented shore.
The high sun cleans out the darkness around
your hoof, and you stop to step over the bruised leaf:
unsighted "conversation" never about the conversation.
Solstice came lashing shadows with scars of light over you, over
the ground.

They heal when the sun goes down.

Petrichor

Pastel blue wash sprays its pattern
across a cloud's skirt of rain.
I cast my breath out from the patio
a soft handed reply:
grass and their tips
slicked with the nutrient musk of citrus,
promising that any war between Heaven and earth
had settled.

Impulse

The impulse to create
is the same call to help people.

Harvest

She fell from a sky garden
I've been watering in my head
since I was a boy.

After I settled for the best
and not just the best I can have.

Her word,
stuck on my shoe,
walked me to a field
where I was filtered through dance
and harvested as her poetry.

Invisible

Illiteracy in intimacy
has left me
invisible.

Astronaut

Her smiles are constellations
as she pours twilight in my Hermes cup.
I grade my resources as reliable and recycled
when I drink down to the alabaster dunes.
I am an astronaut.

I Am of a Desert

I am of a desert.
Abandoned,
wind lulls me into forced migration
to blow me apart into crystal feathers.
Though I am deserted,
I am of a desert
complete
across the earth
or pooled in your hand.

Stories

The sticks on the shore,
the stories they could tell.

I Should Have Taken You to the Beach

You asked me to take you to the beach
I should have taken you.

Nightly,
when the tide takes her reign.
Her fingers overflowing sandcastles, my private defenses
broken down by salt from her womb.

My heart,
cushioned by driftwood
unseals an outward beam to sea,
forgiving the way it used to be.
I haven't touched you in years
but I still feel you.

Mercy

Being alone
offers a mercy
that people can't give.

Coffee

14 hours clockwise on set
at an imaginary pub.
My posture takes prop coffee
to cope with the slump
breaking out of design
becoming authentic.

Marigold on the Windowsill

Tender marigold shielded in soil
your sister magnolia loosens her plates into vanilla petals
piercing the sphere of streetlights
to roll away as the sun comes up.

Her life,
held in sculptor leaflets
meshing back into the earth,
fulfills in decay.

Your colours vein into twilight
blood deepens into clay.

It is not without grief
to be eased into nothingness.
Like the moth consumed
in mourning
waiting for you.

Hook

The hook
always represents someone.
You only know
once you're at the other end of the line.

Ribbon of Babylon

My two feet apart
stepping together into a split second made whole
at the end of a life
my one life.

Naked at first sight
in first light
saturating darkness with definition.
You were ready to be hurt and almost ready to love
so was I.

You saw me through and through
by way of wayward thread,
and I saw you when I read the sunshine on your bare back
pulling moonlight sleeves from your arms
your skin, the clarity of canvas.
I didn't need to try
it just happened.

Falling was flying,
questioning you was challenging you,
knowing you,
was finding me.
My tears moistened by your memories
as you are with me in my own.

My hand wounded at the end of one life
a refuge within another
this is the face that will not be turned away
in the horizon line of your arms
a ribbon around our world.

At One Time

There's nowhere to hide
when I'm shrinking in your palm
after my spirit gave you my body.

Furnace

Longing concealed in downpour
stripped me on the furnace mattress
desire clothed as bareness
hid me underneath sheets.

The bulb flickers
misaligning the future in my head with the present
and in a second long shadow you came to me.

Do you think about me
after I've thought about you?
like the taste lingers
after the tongue has gone lax.

If being afraid is being dampened by sweat
then yes,
I am afraid of salt sticking to collect
while gravity earns its salary of age.
It burns
as much as we've been the same person,
we are not.

Tolerate

So much is wasted
because you tolerate.

Noir

Walking home alone
air grinding out your tongue
streetlights defining expressions on your face
moonlight spills through the cracks down the street
as letdowns laced in spirals.

Obscurity is illumined into the obvious
a vacancy in your hands that so many have filled.
I look for you on this street
and like a hard man smiling at a flower
the aching relevance of my feelings
pulls me back.

Of Age

The home I build
will not be
the house I grew up in.

Smile Lines

If only
days ahead
were always proven to be
as loving as the smile lines
on your face.

The Ink Has Dried

The pen leaks over the page
postcards never sent.
Places you'll never see
landmarks for me
moments thought forgotten
but sensations still felt
where *I love you's* are written in ink.

In one motion I dive in
rolling over to curl my arms around you
wipes the ink from the sheets
stretching through a backward door in time
to tell you that I loved you
but the ink has dried.

Steps

Night.
I'm sitting on my uncle's steps
gazing at powerlines,
the windshield wipers of the sky,
until stars
disappear.

The Fountain by San Lorenzo

Mornings are best.
Plates singing in their afterlife across the cafe floor.
Dozens of confessions conversing quietly under Jobim's guitar.
The sun curate's buildings hourly
as I lounge across from a fountain.
Time and I notice all these things.

Except
a student rubs their dream into a coin
and tosses it in the organic motor
to wish away a toll of uncollected pain.
A mineral parade ripples from this deposit
in ceremony.
The water overflows
with the elasticity of whispers
wading them in an ecosystem
of unpolluted love.

I can hear the written wish
granted by the voice of streams
that time has not noticed.

It is Okay to Cry

I cannot explain.
I cry
though I am as
happy
as yesterday.
No recoil in my palm
pressing against glass on a winter's night.
But today
even with sun,
it is okay
to

cry.

Requests

I wish I could be what you ask
but,
I don't know how to be anybody else.

Last to Sleep

Between me then
and me now
I'm always the last to sleep.

Bankrupt

You said you don't want to lose me
but what I hear is "stay until I find someone else."
Your wealth of words
seemingly go bankrupt.

Attention

My attention
pinned miles deep
in a dark corner of the room.
Dust settled for too long
unwilling to live up to the magic of its past.

The oak bookshelf
hacked by books
I'll never finish.

My legs clogged with stumble
drip downstairs to the mirror,
where your attention goes
sugar skin and leather lips
under concentrated beams
that are never focused.

Where have we gone?

The identity of teardrops
flows from the two-toned pulse
of the human heart.
It is one part familiar with pain.
The other part,
not knowing what to do with it.

Obstacle

Your place in this world is always someone else's obstacle.

Posture

My shadow
sleeps adrift
in postures of daylight
blanketed
under night.

Foliage

This morning,
my hearing crawls
low to the ground,
when ready,
climbs a ladder
foliage to windfall
to branch to
husk.

From this bosom,
wind dances me across the land like
leaves in music.
Mapping out our only signature:
I was here.

Components

We are components of each other's lives,
we're just not always compatible.

Control

Thinking I was in control
was the best way to lose it.

Now
I'm waiting for coincidence to feel like fate again,
a man who only appears as the backdrop he's in.

Dust Bowl

There's no erasing
only burying.
Dirt piles under the guise of shelter
cratering my brows
clouding my eyes
sanding my voice.

A streak of whistle
marks language in sand
from shapeless plains.
If you can read it
you have discovered me.

The space between
words lost and found,
becomes an empty measure
when you dig me up.

Sparkle

The sparkle hides in your eye,
because the rooms you keep finding yourself in
have no light.

Reconcile

I cupped your face,
your cheeks dissolved in a diamond flush.
Reconciling slipping out of disguise,
seizes my past as complete
now that it flows home to you.

Trouble

Stretch your legs
because trouble gets tired
and won't follow you forever.

Sincerity

A room swollen midnight blue
bedroom of many firsts.
I come alone with
heart sewn into the seam of a tight jacket.
Floorboard tracks unwinding here
to this dent of sincerity on sheets.
I promise I will be careful
as I lose myself.

Flight Over Fiume

The face of the cloud
bleached you and I
before sending us on our way.

The afterglow of steel
pales to pearly basins open below.
I flew through them in your eyes
and fell in a cradle of gravity.

We are not of this earth,
when all we have sought
we can touch
when we're both in the sky.

Sunlight

You wear sunlight so well.

Let Him Sleep

Let him sleep
roaming through winter bedded in bone
in reflexes chiseling down the joint.
Lay bare as clay
broken up into cracks
veins stretching wild as faults
combed together in the privilege of sleep.

Let him remold
with his hands pressing
the fortunate pillow,
be it a month or a few years.

Who can say
how long it will take
to step off in dream
what we stepped on
in waking?

The Body

The mind healed
what the body could not
and it forgot
what the body could not.

Siren

Somewhere in your bones is a lover
dreaming aloud in song.
Lean and lush one night lines
unsheathed bare as your collarbone
carving a chance to be a thief.

Yet,
you wrap around my body
like you always belonged there
where nothing is stolen
only hidden
before it's yours.

Tea Leaves

Dismissed to the hotel
to be rescued
to forget.
Bed, sleepless and boiling
after outrunning the hands of the clock
until I was sick.

Rushed to the island
I started picking leaves from porcelain temples.
Every breath thought taken and gone
savored in the grassy rim of my cup.

The question that is my name
stirs in a riddle of medicine
solved in its taking.

Streetlights

There's magic in the moment the streetlights come on.

Lead Balloon

The roar of the walk sign,
putt of the tired exhaust,
a microphone yawn,
construction lullabies
flooding my ears
weighing my head down on the pillow,
a lead balloon.

I roll my head to see
steam flowers blooming.
I almost missed your quiet release.

Passenger

You keep driving
the red light won't see us while it's blinking
while we redraw margins on your palm into patterns.
You know all the rules of the road
inside the terrain of a rose.

You drop me off
and you're far away but distance delays between us.
We become attuned to whispers networking like string
in phone lines, and tire treads
moving like currents across concrete
the freeway slipstream lights.

Bulb

The light in my room burnt out.
Naturally, I thought about you.

Nourishment

"Why didn't you eat breakfast?"
"Because nourishment was sleeping in, next to you."

Hospital

An endless hospital waiting room
alone in your books
chairs you keep warm
with borrowed good news.

Tragedy
told what you hoped
would pass through you
next in line day to day
aches on the odd numbered page
from top to bottom,
and the off-centre hero
can't see where the page turns.

The arm rest grows cold
you've sunk in the black hole of your collar.
You close the book and stand
as a white robe reaper steps forward
in the light of someone
reading you.

Swing Set

I took my pills
you did too.
We are kindest this time of day
hand in hand to mouth.

Your pupil
tempers the coastline of your iris
when I come home a papier-mâché man.

It's safe
the push
the come down.

'My turn'
calls through the dance of chains
that sets you free.

The Brightest Star

Everyone thinks that the star that shines brightest belongs to them.
It does.

Reminder

It's not home
if you need to be reminded of it.

Walking

I can't tell the difference between walking and running
when both get me nowhere.

The Five-Year City

Without the ends of a country or island
the five-year city staggers into nowhere.
Home to no one but unhappy graffiti
drawn with their backs against the wall
cornered by street gangs of cans intoning steely overcast
swelling over beached shipping containers.
I can't quiet it without silencing all of me.
how much longer do I need to stay here?
as my life within marbles is shot
across cobblestone steps
in a trajectory thinning out as a ledge.
I try not to fall.

Us

Time heals all things
changes all things
in you
in me
but not us.

Underground at Midnight

I see you rub your hands
its invisible friction bolts into my palm
walking me into midnight.

Poised undertones flare up in dark drifts
sunlight stranded in the night,
trying to break through and reach us
sparking a luminous passage.

Slow Down

It's all catching up to me
because knowing better
is learning to slow down.

Frontiers

Loneliness takes a seat with you
after everyone leaves before last call
and tells you
those who call him friend
call you 'stranger'.

I jumped the long way from my forehead,
and with me the wallpaper fell down the walls
making do with these things called love
in this land where sunshine and roses were foreigners.

Only now I choose to fly
a loyal cloud covers my head
and I fly through that too,
others hide their secrets underneath them
scared to lose sight of the sun.

It's always about to rain
droplets are virtuous kamikazes
that take me higher
where I find myself
at the foot of your bed
without memory.
Love becomes a sleeping miracle.

I've given everything to the advent mist
and in this place
it can give something back.

Still

Through it all,
you are still you.

End

I ripped a page from the book of forgiveness
and placed it in my book of anger,
then closed it softly.

Inward

I wrote this for me,
not you.
(That's what I tell myself.)